Hi, Worry. Bye, Worry!

Elizabeth Verdick and Olivia Rae

Illustrated by Steve Mark

free spirit
PUBLISHING®

Text copyright © 2025 by Elizabeth Verdick and Olivia Rae

Illustrations copyright © 2025 by Free Spirit Publishing

All rights reserved. No part of this book may be reproduced or transmitted in any form or by any means, electronic or mechanical, including photocopying, recording, or any information storage and retrieval system, without the prior written consent of the publisher, except for brief quotations in critical reviews and certain other noncommercial uses permitted by copyright law. For permission requests, contact the publisher.

Free Spirit, Free Spirit Publishing, and associated logos are trademarks and/or registered trademarks of Teacher Created Materials. A complete listing of our logos and trademarks is available at freespirit.com.

Library of Congress Cataloging-in-Publication Data
Names: Verdick, Elizabeth, author. | Rae, Olivia, author. | Mark, Steve, illustrator.
  Title: Hi, worry. Bye, worry! / Elizabeth Verdick and Olivia Rae ; illustrated by Steve Mark.
  Description: Minneapolis, MN : Free Spirit Publishing, 2025. | Series: Little laugh & learn | Audience: Ages 6–9.
  Identifiers: LCCN 2024039559 (print) | LCCN 2024039560 (ebook) | ISBN 9798885545211 (paperback) | ISBN 9798885545228 (ebook) | ISBN 9798885545235 (epub)
Subjects: LCSH: Worry—Juvenile literature.
  Classification: LCC BF575.W8 .V46 2025 (print) | LCC BF575.W8 (ebook) | DDC 155.4/1246—dc23/eng/20240911
  LC record available at https://lccn.loc.gov/2024039559
  LC ebook record available at https://lccn.loc.gov/2024039560

Lexile® 580L

> Free Spirit Publishing does not have control over or assume responsibility for author or third-party websites and their content. Parents, teachers, and other adults: We strongly urge you to monitor children's use of the internet.

Edited by Eric Braun
Cover and interior design by Colleen Pidel
Illustrated by Steve Mark

Printed by: 465482
Printed in: Malaysia
PO#: 16656

Free Spirit Publishing
An imprint of Teacher Created Materials
9850 51st Avenue North, Suite 100
Minneapolis, MN 55442
(612) 338-2068
help4kids@freespirit.com
freespirit.com

DEDICATION

For every kid who worries—you're not alone!

And for Sonja Solter, a constant shoulder to lean on during life's most challenging times.

ACKNOWLEDGMENTS

Thank you to Eric, for being a great guy and a great guide. And to social worker Deb Dana, who created the term *glimmers* to help people feel better when times are tough.

CONTENTS

CHAPTER 1. Hi, Worry 1

CHAPTER 2. Start Worry-Taming 8

CHAPTER 3. Four Take-Action Tools
for Worries 19

CHAPTER 4. Take Care of YOU
Every Day 40

CHAPTER 5. Handle Big Worries the "Three H" Way 58

CHAPTER 6. Bye (for Now), Worry! 74

Glossary 80

About the Authors and Illustrator 82

Hi, Worry

What do you worry about? We all worry sometimes. Parents worry. So do teachers. So do athletes . . . actors . . . and alligator trainers.

(Authors worry too.)

Everyone worries—no matter how old, how smart, or how strong.

So, what *is* worry?

Worry is that nervous feeling you get from thinking about things that might happen. (Things that seem scary or hard.) These thoughts can BUG you . . . like a buzzing fly. **Zzzzt!**

Worry Can Sound Like . . .

I want to score a goal—can I? What if I don't?

Oh no! I don't know how to do this. Everyone will know!

I have a spelling test today—am I ready? What if I'm NOT?

I need to read aloud in front of the class. What if I make a mistake?

Worry Can Feel Like . . .

Worried thoughts and nervous feelings going round and round can really bring you down. You may feel like this:

Blue

Bleh

Ick

Argh!

BOOM!!!

Maybe you worry about some very serious stuff. Like whether the people in your life are safe and happy. They worry about you too! Remember, all people have these feelings sometimes. **You're not alone.**

You can't avoid worries. But you can learn ways to feel better when they appear. So when a worry pops up, say, **"Hi, worry."**

Then, you'll be ready to try some of the tools in this book. Soon enough, you might be able to say, **"Bye, worry!"**

Start Worry-Taming

Worry has a way of showing up without being invited.

**Knock, knock.
Ding-dong!**

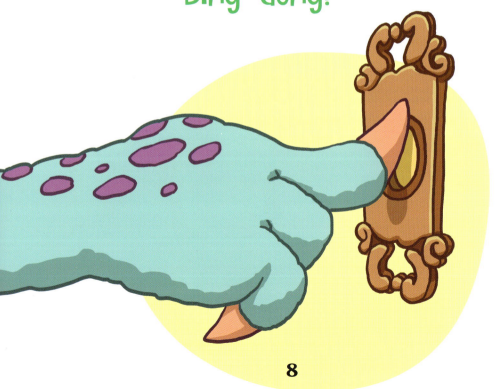

Imagine your worry looks like a T-Rex. She's got big teeth. Tiny arms. And terrible breath.

Your first thought might be, "I'M GETTING OUT OF HERE!"

Instead, **invite** your worry in.

Yes! Because worry wants to tell you something.

Worry Has a Message

Worry is like your very own alert system. Your brain and body are saying, "Hello! Pay attention, please!"

They are telling you to get ready for what's coming up.

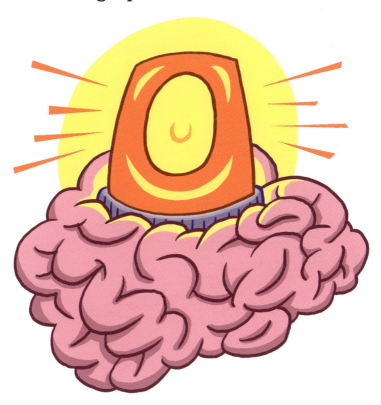

So your . . .

If you know your body's signs, you can tell yourself: **Be ready. Stay steady.**

Ask Worry, "What's Up?"

When worry knocks on your door, open up. You can say: "Worry, I allow you to be here—for now."

To settle yourself down, take **deep breaths**.

Place your hands on your belly. Slowly breathe in through your nose. Slowly breathe out through your mouth. To add some fun, have your lips loosely sealed when you breathe out. Make a fart noise. Farts are funny. Doing something silly can help you deal with worry.

When you're calmer, ask yourself, "What is this worried feeling trying to tell me?"

Try to figure out exactly what you're worried about. Write it down or say it out loud. Putting your worry into words can help. Your worry starts to feel a tiny bit smaller.

Better yet: If you understand *why* you're worried, you can start to do something about it. That's what the next chapter is about.

CHAPTER 3

Four Take-Action Tools for Worries

So, worry's here. And you probably don't want it to stay long—right?

Dealing with worry takes action. This chapter shows you four ways to get going and feel better.

You got this!

TOOL 1
MOVE IT, MOVE IT

Movement helps ease worry. You get your energy flowing in a positive way.

Start with the **Power Stance**. Stand tall with your legs apart. Put your hands on your hips like a superhero. Say, "I am strong enough. I can handle my worries."

And get some exercise! Run at recess. Bike after school. Have a dance party at home.

If you don't have space for big movements, roll your shoulders. Open and close your mouth to let go of worry that sticks in your jaw.

You can also use a fidget of some kind. Focusing on a soothing activity might help you.

Move in any way that feels good to you, so you can shake off worry!

TOOL 2
MAKE ART

When worry strikes, find a way to express who you are and what you feel. This calms your body and brain. Being **creative** also helps you work through big emotions.

So . . .

Write a poem, a rap, or a story.

Make music or dance.

Paint or draw how your worries make you feel.

Act out what you're worried about in the form of a play.

Doodle and write in a journal.

Type your feelings on a computer or tablet.

Write a letter to yourself about what's going on.

TOOL 3
FIND YOUR "LOVES"

When you can tune into what you love, you push the pause button. Your thoughts and breathing slow down. Your worries can go on a break!

Think of your **senses**. *Sight. Sound. Smell. Touch. Taste.* Next, think about things you love. If you like, try this with your eyes closed, taking deep breaths.

Think of three things you love to . . .

SEE

SMELL

HEAR

TOUCH

TASTE

TOOL 4
USE A WORRY JAR

A **Worry Jar** is a place to keep your worries. Get them out of your brain and into the jar.

Write down each worry on a slip of paper. Collect them in a clean jar. Seal the lid to trap them.

Or use a shoebox or an envelope. Decorate your container any way you wish.

Putting your worries away like this means you can come back to them at a later time. When you do, you might see that, in most cases, things turned out okay.

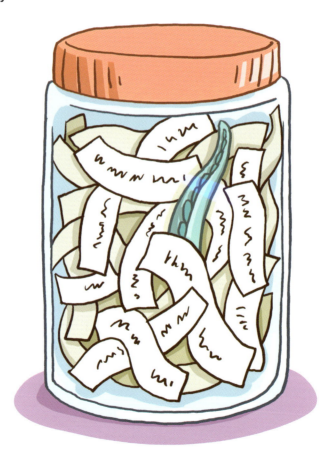

Maybe you felt nervous about your first time on ice skates. Looking back, you may see that you fell a few times but had fun. And you got a little bit better at skating along the way.

Worries happen. But when they do, you can remember all the ways you've learned to stand strong. And you can think back on things you've tried. Maybe you exercised. Or did deep breathing. Or wrote about your worries.

Keep trying! Keep using the tools in this chapter to say "so long" to worry.

TAKE ACTION!
Prepare for What's Coming

Worry may not be welcome. But it's not always the worst. Before that big game or test, worry can give you extra energy. That boost may even help you do better!

Worry can also help you prepare. What if you're worried about your spelling test? Well, maybe your worry is telling you, "Study!"

Or maybe you're worried about your next soccer game. Your worry could be telling you, "Practice!"

Taking action—by studying or practicing—is a great way to tame your worry. You listen to the feeling of "I need to prepare." Then you take steps to get yourself ready. Your time leading up to the game or test is used well.

Whenever you have a worry, ask yourself:

Then figure out if you can do something to prepare for what's coming.

Take Care of YOU Every Day

Think of riding a bike. In order to stay balanced, you have to keep pedaling. But wait, what's this? Big hill ahead!

Life is a little bit like that bike ride. And worries are like hills. If you're **prepared**, you can ride over them.

This chapter is about taking care of yourself so you can handle the hills in life. Even when they're big, steep, winding hills! And the wind is blowing in your face! And there are spiky pits in the road! And *skunks*!

Eat, Sleep, Repeat

Worry can make you feel yucky. When you're worried, you may get an upset stomach. You may not feel hungry. Or you may want to mostly eat food that doesn't give you lasting energy. (Chips! Donuts! Candy!)

Worry can also affect your sleep. Do you stay up late worrying? Wake up in the night with worries on your mind?

All of that can drain your hill-handling power.

But here's some good news! You can take charge when worry sits in your stomach or won't let you sleep.

Eat healthy food.

This gives your body the energy it needs to deal with stress. Try to eat fruits and vegetables every day. Get protein from beans, nuts, eggs, or meat. Avoid foods and drinks that have a lot of sugar.

Kids need about 10 hours of sleep a night. If worry is keeping you awake, here's what you can do:

Start a sleep routine.

Go to bed at the same time every night. About an hour before bedtime, turn off your screens.

Wash up. Read. Talk to a loved one. Pray, if you'd like.

Get Your Quiet Time

Worry can make you feel *too much*. Noises and lights may seem too loud and bright. Your body might get tense.

When you feel like that, try to find some quiet time. Alone.

You could even make a **Comfort Cave**. Use blankets on your bed, in a corner, or under your desk. Turn the lights down low and crawl into your private cave. Now, curl up.

While you're there, take slow, even breaths. This tells your brain "I'm safe" and your body "I'm calm." When you get up, you'll feel a bit calmer.

Be Grateful

Being *grateful* means looking for ways to be thankful. It's called *gratitude*. You can practice gratitude every day.

Take time in the morning or evening to think about what you're grateful for. When you do, life just feels better—and worries feel a little smaller.

Maybe you're grateful for your family, your teacher, or your pet. Or that you had a yummy lunch and got to run around outside. Maybe you're grateful for your friend who always makes you laugh.

You can make a gratitude list every day or week. Share how thankful you are with the people you love.

Look for the Good

If you're worried, keep an eye out for **good things** that help take your mind off your troubles. Notice little things that catch your eye—and your heart. Your cat's purr. Sunlight on your face. A fuzzy caterpillar. Each one is a glimmer. That means it shines.

These small bright things remind you that the world is filled with wonders. Even when you're not worried, try to notice bits of everyday magic.

Keep reading for more ideas for handling the **rough** stuff!

Chapter 5

Handle Big Worries the "Three H" Way

You know that everyone worries. If you were a mind reader, you could hear the worries inside other people's heads. Worries like:

That one's easy enough to solve.

But what about bigger worries? Think about the kind that leave you feeling like you have no control. Especially when the worry is about something you can't change.

Maybe you're worried about a storm. Or about going to the doctor. Maybe you're worried about the first day of school or camp.

You can't stop those things from happening. But you *can* start to tame the worries. HOW?

Get help from someone you trust. You can use the **"Three H" Way**!

Ask yourself, "Do I need to be **heard**, **hugged**, or **helped**?"

Heard

Sometimes, you just need someone to listen. Putting your worries into words can bring feelings of relief. Tell a friend or sibling what you're worried about.

Worries can make you feel lonely. But if you share your worry with someone else, you make a connection. Then you feel less alone. Your buddy may even say, "I worry about that too."

Hugged

Sometimes it takes more than talk to soothe worried feelings. A hug can help.

Hug a family member or friend. If you don't have someone near you to hug, wrap yourself in a cozy blanket. *Squeeze.* A hug or snuggle can make you feel safe.

Or pet a pet! Play with or cuddle a furry friend. Only have a goldfish? No problem. Watch it swim. No pets? That's okay, a stuffed animal can do the trick.

Helped

At times, your worries may be deep or scary. Sometimes they grow and GROW. If that happens to you, tell an adult you're struggling. They can help you feel better.

Who can you talk to? Think of a grown-up you love or trust.

That could be . . .

- A parent or grandparent, or a guardian
- An aunt or uncle
- Your teacher or coach
- Your school counselor or school social worker
- A leader at your place of worship

If you're not sure what to say, one of these ideas can help you get started:

Practice saying these phrases, so they're a little easier when the time comes.

Now you know the "Three H" Way.

Hamster hopes this helps!

TAKE ACTION!
Make a Worry Plan

Dealing with worries is no easy task. Having your tips and tools ready to go when worry shows up can help. Make a worry plan ahead of time. How about right now?

Your worry plan can look however you want it to. You can use this guide:

1. Think of two tools to try when you feel worried.

2. Who can you talk to about your worry?

3. What will you say?

4. Think about how to get some quiet time.

5. Make a gratitude list.

Your plan might look something like this:

When I feel worried, I will try these tools:

1. Write down my worry and put it in my worry jar.

2. Go for a bike ride.

A person I can talk to: Auntie

Some words I can say: Can I tell you about my really hard day?

During quiet time, I will: Chill with my blanket and a good book.

Today I am grateful for: Sunshine and nature

Write down your plan and keep it with you. You can put it in your pocket, your backpack, or your bedside table. Share it with your adult helper (page 66) so you always have support.

CHAPTER 6

Bye (for Now), Worry!

Here's something important to know: Worries come—and worries go.

If you hear that knock on your door, you can be ready.

You can take a breath and say, "Hi, worry."

Then, use the skills you've learned to start to tame your worry. In time, it will pass.

As you grow, you'll still have worries. But you'll also have support!

This book can support you. So can loved ones and friends.

You can support them too. You might notice that a friend seems down—or a sibling looks stressed. When you see worry in someone else, share your worry-taming skills. You could say, "Do you want to be heard, hugged, or helped? I'm here for you."

A healthy lifestyle supports you too. Keep taking good care of yourself. Eat well. Sleep well. Move your body. Talk about what's on your mind.

GLOSSARY

connection: (page 63) when you relate to someone with similar feelings or experiences

fidget: (page 23) an object to keep your hands and mind busy when you're feeling worried

glimmer: (page 57) something in your day-to-day life that makes you feel good

gratitude: (page 52) the feeling of being thankful

protein: (page 45) a nutrient in food that helps you grow and repair your body

relief: (page 62) feeling better

routine: (page 46) a regular practice that helps you stay balanced

soothe: (page 64) to help you feel calm

support: (page 73) help during a difficult time

tame: (page 38) to bring something under control

tools: (page 7) activities that help get something done

About the Authors and Illustrator

Elizabeth Verdick has been writing children's books ever since her daughter was born. And now that very same daughter writes with her! Elizabeth writes a mix of nonfiction and fiction, all with a theme of cheering kids on and helping them live their best lives. She couldn't do this without the help of her devoted office assistants—her lovable dogs.

Olivia Rae is a children's librarian, yoga teacher, writer, and cat rescuer. This is their first book.

Steve Mark is a freelance illustrator and a part-time puppeteer. He lives in Minnesota and is the father of three and the husband of one. Steve has illustrated many books for children, including all the books in the Little Laugh & Learn® series and in the Laugh & Learn® series for older kids.